Proverbs to Live By

A book whose sale's forbidden all men rush to see, and prohibition turns one reader into three.

Italian Proverb

PROVERBS TO LIVE BY

Timeless Words of Wit and Wisdom

Selected by Gail Peterson
Illustrated With Woodcuts by Fritz Kredel

 Hallmark Editions

A proverb is a short sentence based on long experience.

Miguel de Cervantes

The rung of a ladder was never meant to rest upon, but only to hold a man's foot long enough to enable him to put the other somewhat higher.

Thomas Huxley

A man who has work that suits him and a wife he loves has squared his accounts with life.

Friedrich Hegel

The supreme happiness of life
is the conviction that we are loved.

Victor Hugo

Do not remove a fly from your friend's head with a hatchet.

Chinese Proverb

Think not those faithful who praise all thy words and actions, but those who kindly reprove thy faults.

Socrates

Grief can take care of itself, but to get the full value of a joy you must have somebody to divide it with.

Mark Twain

Keep company with good men,
and you'll increase their number.
Italian Proverb

The riches that are in the heart
cannot be stolen.
Russian Proverb

A mile walked with a friend has
only one hundred steps.
Russian Proverb

Friendship will not continue to
the end which is begun for an end.
Francis Quarles

Happiness is a butterfly, which when pursued, is always just beyond your grasp, but which, if you will sit down quietly, may alight upon you.

Nathaniel Hawthorne

He who limps is still walking.
Swiss Proverb

When the ship has sunk everyone knows how she might have been saved.
Italian Proverb

The girl who can't dance says the band can't play.
Yiddish Proverb

We overlook so much happiness,
because it costs nothing.

Anonymous

Wrinkles should merely indicate
where smiles have been.

Mark Twain

An idea isn't responsible for the
people who believe in it.

Anonymous

Facts do not cease to exist because
they are ignored.

Anonymous

The same fire purifies gold and
consumes straw.

Italian Proverb

The future belongs to him who
knows how to wait.

Russian Proverb

When a woman is speaking to you, listen to what she says with her eyes.

Victor Hugo

Tell a woman she is beautiful,
and the devil will repeat it
to her ten times.

Italian Proverb

Joy and sorrow are next
door neighbors.

German Proverb

To live is to change, and to be perfect is to have changed often.

Cardinal Newman

Who is the bravest hero? He who turns his enemy into a friend.

Hebrew Proverb

There is no comparison between that which is lost by not succeeding, and that which is lost by not trying.

Francis Bacon

If you tell the truth, you don't have to remember anything.

Mark Twain

If you go to war pray once; if you
go on a sea journey pray twice;
but pray three times when you
are going to be married.

Russian Proverb

When you can do the common
things of life in an uncommon
way, you will command the
attention of the world.

George Washington Carver

Children have more need
of models than of critics.

Joseph Joubert

When the fox cannot reach
the grapes he says they
are not ripe.

Greek Proverb

Sorrow is a fruit: God does not
make it grow on limbs too weak
to bear it.

Victor Hugo

Burdens become light when cheerfully borne.

Ovid

There is the same difference in a person before and after he is in love as there is in an unlighted lamp and one that is burning.

Vincent van Gogh

Kindness in words creates confidence; kindness in thinking creates profoundness; kindness in giving creates love.

Lao-Tse

Many who are ahead of their time have to wait for it in uncomfortable quarters.

Anonymous

Be at war with your vices, at peace with your neighbors, and let every new year find you a better man.

Benjamin Franklin

It is much easier to be critical
than to be correct.

Benjamin Disraeli

Knowledge without sense is
twofold folly.

Spanish Proverb

One written word is worth a
thousand pieces of gold.

Japanese Proverb

Wise men talk because they have
something to say; fools, because
they have to say something.

Plato

It is the beautiful bird
which gets caged.

Chinese Proverb

Conceit is God's gift to little men.
Anonymous

He who falls in love with himself
will have no rivals.
Benjamin Franklin

A cynic is a man who knows the
price of everything and the
value of nothing.
Oscar Wilde

Those who bring sunshine to the lives of others cannot keep it from themselves.

Sir James Barrie

He who allows his day to pass by without practicing generosity and enjoying life's pleasures is like a blacksmith's bellows—he breathes but does not live.

Sanskrit Proverb

A barking dog is often more
useful than a sleeping lion.
Arabian Proverb

Never let the bottom of your
purse or your mind be seen.
Anonymous

The journey of a thousand miles
starts with a single step.
Chinese Proverb

If you walk on snow you cannot hide your footprints.

Chinese Proverb

You look for the horse you ride on.

Russian Proverb

God did not create woman from
man's head, that he should
command her, nor from his feet,
that she should be his slave, but
rather from his side, that she
should be near his heart.

Hebrew Proverb

It is useless for the sheep to pass
resolutions in favor of
vegetarianism while the wolf
remains of a different opinion.
W.R. Inge

The liar's punishment is not in
the least that he is not
believed, but that he cannot
believe anyone else.
G. B. Shaw

The pebble in the brook secretly
thinks itself a precious stone.
Japanese Proverb

Do not cut down the tree that
gives you shade.

Arabian Proverb

Patience is the key to joy;
but haste is the key to sorrow.

Arabian Proverb

The reward of a thing well done
is to have done it.

Ralph Waldo Emerson

There is no one luckier than he
who thinks himself so.

German Proverb

When your horse is on the brink of a precipice, it is too late to pull the reins.

Chinese Proverb

A single conversation across the table with a wise man is worth a month's study of books.

Chinese Proverb

Soldiers win battles and generals get the credit.

Napoleon Bonaparte

Education is what remains when we have forgotten all that we have been taught.

Marquis of Halifax

That day is lost on which one has not laughed.

French Proverb

Love is the reward of love.

Johann von Schiller

No wife can endure a gambling husband, unless he is a steady winner.

T.R. Dewar

A man who has committed a mistake and doesn't correct it is committing another mistake.

Confucius

Nothing is more highly to be
prized than the value of each day.

Johann Wolfgang von Goethe

If love be timid it is not true.

Spanish Proverb

It is no use to wait for your ship
to come in unless you have
sent one out.

Belgian Proverb

Let your hook be always cast;
in the pool where you least
expect it, there will be a fish.

Ovid

The devil can cite Scripture
for his purpose.

William Shakespeare

You never know what is enough
until you know what is
more than enough.

William Blake

Having a good wife and rich
cabbage soup, seek not
other things.

Russian Proverb

The grand essentials in this life are something to do, something to love, and something to hope for.

Joseph Addison

He who sings frightens away his ills.

Spanish Proverb

They who give have all things; they who withhold have nothing.

Hindu Proverb

Don't marry for money; you can
borrow it cheaper.
Scottish Proverb

Nothing in life is to be feared.
It is only to be understood.
Marie Curie

Who is wise? He who can learn
from every man.
Hebrew Proverb

We make more enemies by
what we say than friends by
what we do.

John Collins

The best place to find a helping
hand is at the end of your
own arm.

Swedish Proverb

An eel held by the tail is not
yet caught.

Anonymous

Happy the generation where
the great listen to the small,
for it follows that in such
a generation the small will listen
to the great.

Hebrew Proverb

He who rides a tiger is afraid
to dismount.

Chinese Proverb

Shun idleness. It is a rust that attaches itself to the most brilliant of metals.

Voltaire

When you jump for joy, beware that no one moves the ground from beneath your feet.

Anonymous

The great thing in the world is
not so much where we stand, as
in what direction we are moving.
Oliver Wendell Holmes

All the beautiful sentiments in
the world weigh less than a
single lovely action.
James Russell Lowell

It takes little effort to watch
a man carry a load.

Chinese Proverb

Genius is one per cent
inspiration
and ninety-nine per cent
perspiration.

Thomas Edison

When the cat mourns for the mouse do not take her seriously.

Japanese Proverb

You cannot prevent the birds of sadness from passing over your head, but you can prevent their making nests in your hair.

Chinese Proverb

Eat vegetables and fear no creditors,
rather than eat duck and hide.

Hebrew Proverb

He saith little that loveth much.

Italian Proverb

Nothing else in the world, not all
the armies, is so powerful as an
idea whose time has come.

Victor Hugo

Fear less, hope more; eat less, chew more; whine less, breathe more; talk less, say more; hate less, love more; and all good things are yours.

Swedish Proverb

Thatch your roof before rainy weather; dig your well before you become parched with thirst.

Chinese Proverb

It's no use going to the goat's
house to look for wool.

Irish Proverb

The man who talks of an unalterable law is probably an unalterable fool.

Sydney Smith

First catch your hare, then cook it.

Anonymous

He who plants thorns must never expect to gather roses.

Arabian Proverb

Proverbs contradict each other.

That is the wisdom of mankind.

Anonymous